Praise for
Do Unto Earth

"A must-read book for everyone who cares about the future of humanity and our planet."

> —**Dr. Ervin Laszlo**, two-time Nobel Peace Prize nominee, recipient of the Goi Peace Prize and International Mandir of Peace Prize, best-selling author of Science and the Akashic Field, founder of the Laszlo Institute of New Paradigm Research and The Club of Budapest, fellow of the World Academy of Art and Science and the International Academy of Philosophy of Science

"A 911 call from Planet Earth herself, *Do Unto Earth* is a potent manifesto for living life today and forward. This book should be required reading in schools. We must act now!"

> —**Mary Madeiras**, three-time Emmy-Winning director, screenwriter, Akashic Records practitioner, activist, and author

"*Do Unto Earth* is full of empowering messages and mind-bending assertions that you won't find in science or history textbooks. Given the urgent need for new solutions on this endangered planet, the ideas are worthy of further investigation."

—**Mark Gober**, author of *An End to Upside Down Thinking*, board of directors of the Institute of Noetic Sciences (IONS) and the School of Wholeness and Enlightenment (SoWE)

"From page one, I was hooked! *Do Unto Earth* merges spirituality with our environmental crisis and does it in a way that is as gripping as a blockbuster movie. Brava to Hayes, Borgens … and Pax."

—**Temple Hayes**, author, spiritual leader, animal activist, and founder of illli.org

"The channeled Spirit energy Pax states that we are at the 'crossroads of our survival' and offers us bold envisioning and direction. Mother Earth is speaking, and ancient mysteries are revealed! Let's heed and implement these game-changers for the benefit of us all."

—**Sunny Chayes**, social/human rights and environmental activist, feature writer and Chief Strategic Partner for Whole Life Times, and host of ABC's *Solutionary Sundays*

"Timely, high-level and generative wisdom detailing how we may still sustain our beautiful planet while reclaiming our collective and individual sovereignty."

—**Stephan McGuire**, director of Zürich-based NGO Cernunnos Media, Director of Tree Media Foundation

Pax and the Journey to New Worlds

Pax and the Journey to New Worlds

Volume 8 of Do Unto Earth

PENELOPE JEAN HAYES,
CAROLE SERENE BORGENS

Waterside Productions

Cover design by:
Andrew Green
Books & Illustration

Printed in the United States of America

First Printing, 2020

ISBN-13: 978-1-951805-13-5 print edition
ISBN-13: 978-1-951805-14-2 ebook edition

Waterside Productions
2055 Oxford Ave
Cardiff, CA 92007
www.waterside.com

For you—
so you know for certain that you are the change and
you have the power

Contents

Introduction · xi

Volume 8 · **1**
Do Unto Earth   **Pax and the Journey
                    to New Worlds** · · · · · · **1**
Chapter Twenty-Six: Other Planet
                         Colonization · · · · · · · · · · 3
Chapter Twenty-Seven: Interstellar Travel at
                         Lightspeed · · · · · · · · · · · 15
Chapter Twenty-Eight: The Secret Lives of
                         Extraterrestrials · · · · · · · 26
Chapter Twenty-Nine: A Place in Time · · · · · · 58

About the Author and Channeler· · · · · · · · · · · · · · 81

Introduction

Do Unto Earth is an extraordinary conversation intended to quantum leap us forward in our spiritual evolution and journey to enlightenment. This message is not a directive delivered from a thousand feet up; this is a very personal message from and dialogue with the Divine Wisdom Source directly to you and for you. Please accept this gift with eyes clear and wide and open.

Within these pages is the blueprint for environmental repair and peace and unity on Earth, however, this booklet constitutes just one of eight volumes that together make up that blueprint. While we believe that the eight topics, as separated by these volumes, are to be understood as connected to each other and only together give the full message as intended, we also understand some readers prefer to focus on their specific areas of interest—hence these eight mini-books by volumes. (Note: Chapters within this volume are numbered as they originally appeared in the book's full-length version.)

As you begin this journey, you might like to know how this collaboration of writing began.

It is indeed my great joy and honor to communicate with the Spirit Messenger, Pax, channeled by Carole Serene Borgens. From a young age, Carole, a former nurse, diligently studied all things metaphysical. This Spirit Messenger first visited her in the early 1990s when she was new to channeling by automatic writing. When her pen wrote the opening introduction and request for her to be a channel, she recognized the profound responsibility attached and jumped up from her office chair to pace the floor—not easy with three sleeping Irish Wolfhounds covering the carpet. Carole's initial response was to ask if she could think about it and take some time to respond, which she was given. Asking, "Why me?" Spirit responded to her: "You are new to this, you have no bad habits, and you will change none of my words." In time, Carole came to be comfortable with this blessing and so began her journey.

I, too, have been a seeker and spiritualist since my years as a teenaged runaway, and so it is a useful tool at times for me to reach out to a reputable intuitive for deeper guidance. Beginning on the fourth of February 2019, I had several long-distance Spirit channeling sessions with Carole—she was in British Columbia and I was in Florida. I had copious questions for Spirit as I sought further direction for my second title, *Do Unto Earth* (which, incidentally, is also the name of my business), while building upon the message of my first title, *The Magic of Viral Energy*. I was expanding and broadening the message of "viral energy" from personal and interpersonal goals to global concerns facing humanity and Planet Earth. I was also simultaneously establishing the Viral Energy Institute, a learning and research platform for the study of Viralenology.

Through our talks, this Spirit Messenger and I were getting to know each other and Spirit felt my passion for the plight of abused animals and species extinction, as well as my intention to bring awareness to our environmental crisis and to share the impacts of "viral energy masses"—large energetic fields created by both light and heavy intentions and action by communities, populations, industries, governments, and cultural beliefs—on Planet Earth. These disruptive energy masses create massive vibrational pockets of particular energies including love, hate, peace, discord, gratitude, violence, forgiveness, indifference, and compassion.

The Spirit Messenger seemed very interested in this direction and before long, Carole contacted me to say that Spirit wished to offer wisdom to be used by and shared through the Viral Energy Institute regarding this mission of planetary healing.

The writing began on the second of October 2019 when I sent questions to Carole who then channeled Spirit's responses by automatic writing (today, she does this via typing). It was *during* the writing that it became clear to all that this conversation would take book form and adopt the title *Do Unto Earth*.

As the answers were returned from Spirit, Carole and I both had many moments of excitement and more than a few gasps followed by, "Ooooh crikey, this is going to change everything!" The first of such revelations came in Chapter One when I asked the Spirit Messenger (whom self-identified with the moniker

"**Pax**", meaning peace) to be more specific about who they are. Here was the answer...

> "**We are one with the Universe, not the Universe alone. We are the Divine Universe, yes, and the God being and the greater wisdom, that which knows and supports all and is healing, non-judgmental and tolerant, all-seeing, all-knowing, and Peace.**"

Volume 8

Do Unto Earth
Pax and the Journey to New Worlds

"Our only chance of long-term survival is not to remain inward-looking on Planet Earth, but to spread out into space."

Stephen Hawking

Theoretical physicist, cosmologist, winner of the Albert Einstein Award, director of research (until death) at the Centre for Theoretical Cosmology at the University of Cambridge

Chapter Twenty-Six

Other Planet Colonization

*P*ax, how do people find balance between Earth repair and our journey to explore elsewhere?

Oh yes this is the question—how to find balance now with continuing efforts to clean Earth's environment while also forging ahead with space exploration. It is a balance of thinking as well as acting. It is a placing of emphasis and importance on both, simultaneously. How do your people think now about the need to maintain clean Earth while following the need to branch out to space exploration; where is the emphasis, the priority?

In our view of your world and people it seems that not much thought has been given to this question. Of course, it would be that emphasis is placed on getting through one day at a time, family and career and health and wellness, all which demand attention and focus. Most of your Earth people do not give attention to the question of this priority, this inclusion of space travel into their daily thoughts and actions. How is it to be that a question of this magnitude could enter the daily thought process of those simply trying to put food on the table and keep a paying job? It is not a priority.

When we enter into colonization of another habitable planet, will it be people with money and power that go first, and will greed and the need for power be factors that work against peaceful co-existence?

Well, it is the case that there will be an effort to introduce the need for purity of heart and thought among those first explorers. There is a division between settlers and those enabling the journey and settling, and there is opportunity to create a haven for those of pure intentions—in this way it is "utopian" in description and intention.

The power of intention among those facilitating this journey and this settling will serve to bring a higher vibration to those involved and endeavor to raise the project to one of purity of intention.

We understand that you will be grateful for our guidance in this colonization journey and we, together with others of high-mind and experience in the Spirit realm, will continue to advance our support and ideas.

It's inspiring and very emotional to know that help is coming.

And this is how it is.

For those who will pursue other planet colonization, what planet is the best option?

When it is considered time to colonize another planet, that new home will show itself. At present there is no knowledge of where or how to journey there, and not enough time to undertake a journey for most.

It breaks my heart to think of abandoning Planet Earth; she is so beautiful and blue and green, and I couldn't imagine a better alternative for us than to heal Earth and commit to her.

Seeking peace on your planet should be top of mind, not just how to leave it. Is it your people's belief that leaving for another planet will be a solution; that only the good and peaceful people will be transported? Reality is not so. Reality is that energy, healing energy, must now be utilized to clear greed and avarice on your planet. These are the basis of all warring. If there were a method now for your peoples to move to another planet, they would be "running away" from the poor conditions they have created on Planet Earth. In "running to" an alternative home, those who created the unfavorable conditions on Earth will simply relocate and resume their habits elsewhere. How long do you think this idyllic new home will be idyllic? First, heal yourself.

While we work to clean up Earth, can we also plan for colonizing another planet or must we complete our clean up first?

At the current rate of your planet's demise, it is desirable to make a Plan B for future generations: to speak of colonizing other planets is to reflect that which we have spoken of. There will be no clean air, water, or soil within one and a half generations, so how does the Earth population plan to eat, breathe, and survive?

This is not an idle threat—it is reality. There is already too much damage done to save all of the planet and populating of others will occur in the next generation.

Ouch. Colonization of another planet will become a *need* for humans?

The end of civilization on Planet Earth is a potential, of course, and there seems already a way around that with plans to colonize other planets while repairing this one: this should successfully avoid cataclysm. As your time shows poisoning of earth soils and air and water, continuing to support population at current levels is a challenge.

For those intrepid souls who seek to forge ahead with development of civilization elsewhere, transportation and methods in current development support travel to another planet to colonize, farm, and grow in readiness for increased population arrival.

This is done to relieve pressure on Planet Earth while repair is underway. It is the need to rehabilitate your Earth, not abandon her, so those who wish to travel and be pioneers and homesteaders on another planet will gladly do so. They forge ahead in the making of new lives and civilization, while those wishing to remain to repair Earth, will do so.

Earth people do travel off-planet to begin new civilization(s) elsewhere.

We have said that the need to remove large portions of your population to alternate locations exists, but the transport means do not as of yet. While they are being created on your Earth plane, they exist in heightened sophistication in civilizations elsewhere, off-planet.

Do you consider the possibility of combining the need with the resource? Can your Earth population see themselves entering the unknown in this way? Explorers and pioneers and those with no fear of striking out on their own to begin again elsewhere—these people exist.

That there is not yet infrastructure at the destination is a present-day situation and will change in your soon time. You have a space-station structure, but this is not what will be the home-base: it is a solid and on-land structure. If eating and breathing and life-functions can now exist on a space-station, a dedicated-to-the-process solid structure, situated on solid ground, can be constructed to host the explorers.

There is much to consider and much to be divulged of your Earth science as it has progressed in this direction but not been divulged to the public. We know and we share and there will be nonbelievers as well as those asking where they can sign-up.

It's now time to focus on interstellar travel and the colonization of an alternative home for Earth people while refreshing Planet Earth.

Does the plural in "colonize other planets" and "new civilization(s)" mean that we will set up a number of colonies on more than one other planet?

Oh yes, you will look to go big and colonize more than one planet.

To find suitable hosts, however, will take time but meanwhile there is exploration and preparation to be done.

Your science prepares propulsion methods to get you there as well they prepare ideas for supporting life on arrival.

There is no known destination at this time that duplicates Earth and will be the most like your present home, but that will come. First is the transport means to get there as well as a sense of where it may be that your next home is located.

The pieces do come together as the many branches of science work to answer the questions around this great undertaking. As your time progresses there is renewed energy put into this study and greater commitment by people to join the science making it become reality.

One step at a time and one day at a time and it will be.

To live inside a space station on a grey and life-barren planet sounds bleak to me. Are there no other beautiful blue and green planets accessible to us now?

Space travel time and distance determine the where, and your science determines the when. While there may be these twin planets—their existence in your galaxy or elsewhere is not yet known (to your people) nor is the method to visit. There will be no awareness of soon-time travel to a duplicate of Planet Earth, no, as planetary locations relative to your Earth Sun make it unlikely. Farther removed, however, there will be, even though not accessible at this time. It is not to be a focus of your current Earth science.

You will find alternatives closer and as technology catches up with need, those afar may be explored. For now, it remains a journey into technology and alternatives and time will bring the ways needed to undertake this adventure.

I guess there are some people who are into the lifestyle of living on a space outpost firmly planted on a life-barren planet, but I don't see the appeal. I like landscapes with waterfalls to

admire and mountains to hike. I like peacefully paddling down quiet rivers, and hearing the birds chirp in the morning and again at night. I like the changing seasons and the smell of fresh rain on summer-hot terra.

Will the settlers of such a planet-station live indoors their whole lives, perhaps creating faux-outdoor spaces but never again knowing the reality of a living and lush planet?

This is dependent upon the destination chosen. Those who are comfortable with isolation from nature will be accepting. As there are city people and country people, there are choices to be made.

We do not describe all future planetary homes at this time as they are yet to be identified and chosen. Choices exist, or they *will.*

Those who travel off-planet initially are less concerned about the destination, and more about the journey.

I see—they'll do it for the adventure, the newness, the intrigue, and the science of it. Yet, for those like me who are enamored with a lush and living planet home, I suspect that you'd say that we should clean up Earth and take care of her if we love her so much. Of course, I'm with you on that.

In your world today is deep unrest and upheaval. It will begin to heal, yes, but in order to effect repair there must be not only awareness but the bravery of speaking up and speaking out, in peace, to what will regain integrity and purity of the heart of your nations around the globe. Some are there and some are close while others have driven themselves over the cliff and require a complete rebuild in order to function in integrity.

The mist is lifting and now you could not be clearer as to why this book's various topics are to be understood together: like the ingredients in a recipe that must be mixed together to create the desired outcome. All topics here are related to environmental repair. The eight subjects of *Do Unto Earth* are not separate topics at all, are they Pax? Together this is a complete message that says: Do unto Earth as you would have Earth do unto you!

Yes.

We ask that your people trust in their own voices to speak their truth to power and ensure forward motion for your humanity and not only for survival but to flourish once again as peaceful societies in respect and love for all.

We wish also to speak of resettling and new beginnings and the old ways brought forward to form the basis for new society. There is the moving to explore another planet with a view to settling. Preliminary work now being done in this direction shows promise and we can build on this.

Adding in assistance from those intergalactic supporters of old will bring an interesting twist and allow for a progressive journey into what-ifs and what is possible. Our friends from afar show the way, if permitted, to refreshing your ways and re-establishing a healthy Earth society.

Will ETs make an in-person visit to help and guide us?

In this present incendiary society as a whole on your Earth plane, not a visitation for the purpose in sharing wisdom for your future is possible. To which unsettled country would they aim and into which warring culture would they insert themselves with an offer so out of the realm of expected and logical sounding messages? Your planetary cultures are fractured and worsening and to think a peaceful entry into your world is possible at this place in time is not reality. The fear this would bring to your peoples and the intent to capture for their own future gain would be forefront in behavior and will not be undertaken as a result. There will be no further intentions to bring friendly and helpful visitations until your warring and greed and wish to maintain supremacy changes into your people developing confidence and empowerment to the extent they cease to fear what may be offered to them in peace. It just will not be.

Can we access their wisdom through our conversations, yes, and we will fill our energies for a time preparing Earth peoples to listen, to purify their own thinking and acting, to be caring about your climate crisis, and commit to behavioral changes that result in a wave of energy toward the repair of your planetary resources.

(Well, this answers the Fermi paradox.)
Will our next planet be a place of unity, peace, and bliss?

Well it is ours to say that "Utopia" is a state of mind, is it not? It is not a place and perfection is in the view of the individual and the judgment of that individual. It is not—outside of a fairy-tale—practical to think your world will rise to this description, either on Planet Earth or your next destination home. Your people carry corruption and greed, and this will not be eradicated within the next generation or two. There is much work to be done by your people and perfection won't be reality until this is undertaken, if ever. The creation of a "utopian home place" is represented by the introduction of peace and prosperity for all—these are not present on your current Earth plane.

A new home of the old and proven ideas for peaceful co-existence in a future time and place is the way.

Is Earth the fairest planet in the Universe (to put it in Magic Mirror terms) or are there other beautiful and life-filled planets out there?

Such places exist, yes, and in the eternal darkness of space, unexplored mostly at your time and place in existence, there are host planets that may be considered in your future. Vast in nature and vital in make-up, they could support life as you know it.

The immensity of space brings challenges to travel of course and this will be surmounted by your science, in time, with help from *future* technology as previously discussed.

"*Eternal darkness*" …hmmm, I'm a bit concerned by our people's history of easily getting the message screwed up or attaching fear to it. While I know the difference between light (such as perceived by the sense of sight and an energy byproduct) and Light (as in enlightenment and highly vibrating intention-energy), and dark (as in the dimness of the visual sense of light) and dark (such as polluted intention and action which clouds the Light of goodness), others might require your reference of "eternal darkness" to be made crystal clear in context before they go off in the wrong direction with the message.

Eternal darkness is deep space. Not gloom and doom and fear darkness, and is to be interpreted as such. It is deep space your people wish to access. You may refer to the locations of habitable planets as the great unknown or the unexplored, but we suggest it is as we have stated: the eternal darkness of deep space which shall be illuminated by your finding and visiting them.

Chapter Twenty-Seven

Interstellar Travel at Lightspeed

You've said that "our friends from afar show the way" in our project of exploring another planet's colonization. I'd love to know who is on the team! Who are the ET friends who will show us the way?

As your science becomes able to replicate the technology which brought visitors to your Planet Earth in past, the speed at which the project flows increases. Your military and government are aware of the history, location of classified records, and details of the transport vehicles used and reverse-engineered following crashing to Earth.

These records exist and only those in power know why or if they will remain secret.

Are you speaking again of the spaceship still held and locked up in secrecy at Area 51—the craft that crashed at Roswell?

Oh yes, it is so.

Has this craft been fully utilized in our ability to reverse-engineer, or is there still more technology and wisdom that can be uncovered from this craft by re-opening the records and vaults?

All that is known and has been learned can benefit by additional looks as technology continues to grow and advance toward what is there. Recognition of what is there will grow as your technology does and is understood.

The value is in continual inspection and comparing with what is currently known and what is in development.

I would imagine that reverse-engineering the craft would provide information about the vehicle's engine and propulsion system, yet I'm not sure it would explain how to harness the no-fuel propulsion source. And, even if our government intelligence and military has unearthed (ha!) from this craft all that is needed to reproduce the technology and no-fuel energy source to run it, this information is not disclosed to the public; it's kept in secrecy. As businessman J.P. Morgan infamously expressed to Nicola Tesla—if they can't put a meter on it, they don't want it.

Pax, will fuel one day be free?

Yes.

You've told us that the no-fuel energy source is a method not a product: it's free energy and will change everything from pollution to carbon emissions, and it will upset the geo-economic system, open new industries, end secrecy and corruption, and eliminate the 1% (or perhaps the .001%) from holding society's power. It will essentially end the monetization of energy as a meter-monitored paid utility. And, it will allow for interstellar travel at lightspeed.

It also would mean the end of oil, coal, nuclear, public utilities, and even solar and wind power (which, while largely clean, are still monetized utilities like all the rest).

In addition, the open source energy method would shift the power from the very few with special interest and re-seat power with the entire population of the world.

Pax, the no-fuel propulsion source, if known by some, is not going to be released by our governments because they are tied to the stakeholders of big oil and the like. The suppression of clean, free, and equitable energy will continue unless We The People get a divine intervention or some extraterrestrial help.

Of course, there will be no interstellar travel without the means to get there by lightspeed and beyond, and so let's begin to talk about the propulsion systems used by our interstellar supporters.

Pax, what can you tell us?

The spark of energy needed to propel and maintain space flight and travel is the catalyst, and that is known and being developed by space researchers now. It will be shared with those developing the technology both in public and private enterprise.

The energy is harnessed from deep space and this will become more known as science progresses.

I believe you're talking about Dark Matter. Crikey, Pax.

Time allows for continual recognition and inspiration to identify and unravel mysteries.

Some of our famous physicists from history such as Nicola Tesla and Hendrik Casimir brought in the idea of Dark Energy being a zero-point energy field: pulling energy from the quantum vacuum. Is the zero-point energy field the secret behind interstellar travel propulsion systems?

Partially, and it is currently in laboratory trials—the ability to promote and deliver a method of propulsion for space travel that is independent of fossil fuel use on your Earth plane. There is no means for storing liquid fuel in sufficient quantity on board a space travel vehicle that will serve a purpose designed for lengthy travel and return.

Dark Matter is something (or no thing) that our cosmologists still know practically nothing about.

Here's what we do know: Dark Matter does not emit, absorb, or reflect light, and yet we know that it has a gravitational impact because it bends light as it passes nearby. It is something, it has an impact, it is a force or power. Beyond that, it's a mystery to us and I can't help but ask for some enlightenment on this from the Spirit World.

What precisely is Dark Matter?

It is a place, emptiness, and a non-place all at once. It is a nowhere and an everywhere, a void to be filled? What is and what is not are in this void and it will become useful in time.

"It will become useful in time"—well, well, how compelling.

Let's start more broadly. Dark Energy/Dark Matter does not contain matter?

It is the great void of magnetic being that results in swirling masses of energy. We suggest that this is a *place*, this Dark Energy, and it is of interest to those in the scientific community for its potential to hold secrets.

When the time is right there will be exploration of these places that results in the demystifying of all things related to space. For now, it is the darkness of knowledge that remains.

It is deep space. It is the place in the time.

When Dark Energy is understood, *all* mysteries of space will be revealed/known?

All mysteries will never be completely revealed as time passing creates more mysteries within the Universe. We may say that as humankind is ready for the revealing, it will be. *As we have stated, when the time is right.*

Is Dark Energy the last frontier of exploration?

At this time when focus is on what lies within Dark Energy, it will seem as though it is a last frontier. As the Universe continues to move boundaries over time, there will always become another frontier for exploration. At this time there is no final frontier.

Does Dark Energy expand?

Expansion and contraction is, and as it is, the density varies. Like stretching taffy, it can be smaller and thicker or greater and thinner. Where lies the strength do you think?

This is a puzzle for our cosmologists and theoretical physicists.
Does Dark Matter/Dark Energy have *intelligence*? If so, *who* (or what) is the cosmic mind behind this intelligence of Dark Energy?

We are here to say this is not the application for these places in time.

Be aware of the placing of these areas and their intention as part of the Universe.

Separate time from place from intelligence and it will be clear.

(More breadcrumbs. *The placing. Their intention.* Maybe the locations of Dark Energy are connected to their purpose and function in the Universe.)

You have referred to Dark Matter as anti-gravity and that its usefulness to us would be revealed in time. May you please expand on Dark Matter's origins and purpose?

This is the *weightless* and almost *indefinable energy* found in corners of unexplored space and it will contribute to your wellness when understood and harnessed. It is the void and the place of worship for the many. How is this meant, you ask? Those cosmologists who try to understand and control indefinable areas of space do worship at the altar of higher learning and endeavor to communicate with who and what may be present there. It is for them to continue the focus and the in-depth search.

May you please speak to a zero-point quantum vacuum system and how we can utilize this zero-point energy source?

This is a necessary forward motion in the space travel industry and together with science brings forward an integrated fuel system. The ability of some to integrate systems and take from each what will blend and meld and contribute to the whole is underway and the end result shows itself in your soon time.

I've been doing my research so that I might ask the pertinent questions, and I've learned that our scientists have produced models and theories to explain the way in which the zero-point field works, however there is still a missing piece of knowledge. Some scientists say that the problem is (and I'm paraphrasing and summarizing to the best of my understanding) that they can't yet figure out how to interrupt the quantum field in order to extract some of the energy. Basically, because the field is a balanced bubble there is no pressure differential, and without that the tremendous energy contained inside is just a moot point: it's not useable while held in the balanced field because no pressure means that the power within is powerless (to us anyway).

It seems that our scientists are trying to replicate the zero-point field and figure out how to properly interrupt the quantum vacuum and therefore utilize particles of energy to create the thrust needed to power propulsion systems/engines capable of interstellar travel at the speed of light, or faster.

How do we replicate the zero-point energy field—that tremendous power contained in Dark Energy—in order to use it as the no-fuel power source?

We say it is not for you to replicate but rather to *harness* this—no need to reinvent the wheel.

Then, this means that we harness it in space as opposed to creating it on Earth through man-made energy generation. (This is a giant clue.)

It's believed by some scientists that the zero-point energy field is effectively used for interstellar vehicle travel (perhaps in addition to use as the no-fuel spark of propulsion) because it basically creates a spacetime bubble around the vehicle.

What do you know about the concept of the vehicle creating its own anti-gravity environment which essentially renders it massless?

You might say so, yes, and if this is the technology to strive for then it is achievable. At speed this becomes reality and eases the way forward. It also provides protection somewhat against exterior injury. An energy field surrounding a capsule can deflect potential harm as it travels through space.

Aye aye, Captain.

Some scientists say that extraterrestrial interstellar vehicles are operated by trans-dimensional physics, meaning that they cross through other

dimensions to get here (to Earth) or other places in the Universe. Is this true?

It is, indeed, as the trans-dimensional aspect of it does create forward motion in propulsion. This is an internal fission and fusion, and these together work in tandem for propulsion. This is to be discovered and tested further and will be the way of it.

Until that time, we share that the off-planet trajectory now is to deep space, and this is where the technology is required.

And so, the big question is: *how* can we harness Dark Matter in space?

Harnessing Dark Matter in space is to be a continual study as it is not yet your time to so do. There are steps forward not yet identified and so we suggest that as science further explores space it will become clear.

There is a time for everything in your development and even in your old days it was known that the cart was not placed in front of the horse if forward motion was the goal.

In summary, we use Dark Energy while in space and harness it in space. And so, this leaves the question as to how we get into *deep* space in the first place where we can harness Dark Energy for propulsion whilst in space.

Oh, yes. It is the case that off-planet exploration will become every-day in Earth people's future. In order to get into deep space there are many details yet to be ironed out, and many explorations of technology to be completed. At this time, we point you toward fission and fusion. Your science understands this now as it is the means of current travel. It is our intention to show your people the way of the future, yours not ours, as off-planet people know this technology and use it to buzz by your planet regularly. It is the science of motion put into play and combined with the spark of non-fuel, completes the circuit.

It's an electrical circuit at work, that kind of spark, and together with thrust and propulsion equates to forward motion. It is the simple action of current passing through that creates the fusion which allows the fission and the rest is projected upward. We should like to say it is not rocket-science, but in fact it is. (*Cosmic wink.*)

Chapter Twenty-Eight
The Secret Lives of Extraterrestrials

*L*et's reveal or dispel some alien life and otherworldly enigmas.

In searching for a word to call the peoples of extraterrestrial civilizations, would we call them "people", "humanoids", "aliens", or "beings"?

Well, they answer to many names it seems, and "visitors" is one, "watchers" is another, "supporters" another, and OPA's another (off-planet ancestors). ETs cover the differences between them.

You've told us that our ancient ancestors do not visit us anymore and they don't buzz by to check on us. Rather, it's *other* extraterrestrial supporters who have taken up this role of monitoring our planet and peoples. In terms of the difference between them, would it make sense that the beings who Starseeded us

are OPAs while ETs encompass *all* interstellar beings inclusive of our visitors, ancestors, and those others with whom we've had no contact or history at all?

Do I correctly understand this?

Semantics is the carrier of clarity and this description can be used, yes.

Do all extraterrestrial beings have the same basic physical appearance with two legs, two arms, a torso, and a head etc. (Even if some have larger heads and almond-shaped eyes, and others don't?) Or, are there some OPAs that look like a cross between an *animal* and a human? (Like a lizard-man or something else from our science fiction.)

Science-fiction indeed—no references to lizards exist at this time.

There are differences and there are similarities in their make-up based on their functional needs. A similar type body, although differing in size is correct. Heightened senses, of course, and less dependence on vocal cords for example also differentiate them. Think of the advancements and needs of their existence and the evolution of their bodies and senses complements it.

I guess they don't use their vocal cords if they telepathically communicate. That makes *sense*.

We share that they are not so different from your Earth people in their wishes for peaceful existence while being very different in their intolerance for the darkness of behaviors among your Earth masters, political and industrial.

I wonder if some of our moviemakers are divinely or interstellar-ly inspired?

Is there any basis of truth in our movies such as *E.T. the Extra-Terrestrial* (1982) directed by the sci-fi visionary Steven Spielberg, and/or *Avatar* (2009) directed and produced by the great James Cameron?

We say it is the case that these individuals have the gift of seeing and knowing what is to come through their own sense of radar and sonar and other advanced traits they are blessed with. The tuning in to higher frequencies is their gift and their willingness to mind-transport to download what they see as the bigger picture, is a gift. This they use for seeing what may be and what will be and weaving these perceptions into their stories. It is based on truth and as we know—the truth is out there.

Did they come to these pictures and stories accidentally or were they inspired as a result of Higher-Self-communication? Is it to be believed that their imaginations were unaided in these understandings? We say those who attain a higher level of spirituality see what others don't and receive what others don't by way of what is to come, and these are fine examples.

Indeed, they are.

I'd like to ask you about crop circles. This is one of our mysteries surrounded by significant conjecture. Though many crop circles have been manmade, many others are still unresolved conundrums.

Pax, were any of the crop circles made by aliens? If so, why?

Indeed they are and are done so to send messages as well as to announce their presence and ability to do so. Much is done in a playful manner by those who buzz by, just because they can, and if the humor is to be understood, it is to pique the curiosity of Earth people—mission accomplished!

Ha! Playful aliens: this is about the most amusing thing I can think of!

It is their intention to send a message that they are nearby.

Humor is shared by most species and they are one.

Well, then, I believe the question should follow (because we've not been able to work it out): *how* do they make those crop circles—with what equipment?

Blowers, big blowers that thrust down blasts from their ships and flatten terrain is how.

Aimed in different directions it creates patterns and the view they have while making this art, and they consider it art, gives them the ability to manage small details.

There are elements of radiation and other-world gasses that contribute to the make-up of the thrusting tool.

It is a joy for them to paint their pictures in this way while not harming anyone or anything—like spending the night in an art class it is.

I'm in love with this! I can almost hear a symphony orchestrated to complement this scene. I just can't get enough of this image of jocular and artistic aliens making their crop circles. It's ironic and magical and elegant, and yes—funny!

I would guess that the blowers are not just for making art in wheat crops. What is the primary function of the blowers?

These are the thrusters that allow for propulsion and reverse thrusters also, stopping must be considered. There are variations on these in operation and they function in numerous ways.

When these craft move through time and space, they do so in different trajectories than your earthly airplanes, therefore their requirement for the ability to change pitch and speed and direction in nanoseconds makes them unique in your way of building.

And do they "blow" the regular air atmosphere from outside the craft, or do the blowers blow something that originates from *inside* the craft?

Outside air is rearranged to allow for progress, and systems from within the craft mix with this outside air to complete the picture. It is the fact that the mix of materials creates a composition of metallic nature that touches the Earth field to change the composition of the area. It can be traced that foreign intervention has taken place.

It is a signature like those found on an artist's canvas, but not visible.

"A composition of metallic nature that touches the Earth field." I'm repeating this for emphasis. (Calling all engineers!)

To explore more of the alien arts—do they have music?

Well yes, it is the case that there is music, which to them is not your music sounds nor would it necessarily be pleasing to you. It plays in each operating system for each being, and theirs is the pleasure *as they create it*.

Come again? I want to make sure I'm getting this. What is "each *operating system* for each being"? Is their operating system their brain or nervous system or their cell memory? Or, do they

have a computer inside them, as the term "oper-ating system" would indicate to us?

Ah yes, and that *some* are programmed for specific tasks indicates an operating system. And no, they are not robotic even with this variation to the theme of upright, two-legged intelligence.

You knew I would ask.

Yes.

As a hybrid they vary from both but accomplish similar tasks. There are those that are task-specific, purpose-built, and they contain the artificial intelligence referred to.

A hybrid type of ET with artificial intelligence built in—I'll have to think on this one for a while.

There are levels of intelligence, and there is artificial intelligence, also, which serves a purpose that is useful and decreases numbers of task-managers in a crew in travel. Isn't it interesting to think in this manner, where you can have a hierarchy with leaders and workers, and how does this deviate at all from your current military with officers and grunts as they were once called?

It is the case that these helpers are artificial intelligence to the extent they are task-specific and happy about it. There is no intention to become more and this makes them valuable in the team.

But, they're *not* robots?

Not being robotic is a part of the joy. They are part of the team in place and choose to remain in their place in the hierarchy.

That they experience joy is a nice thought.

There are levels of action and responsibility and "humanoid intelligence"—all are intended to do no harm to Earth populations.

Are aliens considered "humanoid intelligence"? I'm trying to understand this reference as we discuss ETs.

"Humanoid intelligence" is that which is *recognized* by humans and relating to their own. This is not identical nor is it close, but there are similarities sufficient to be recognizable. There are variations within intelligence that will or will not include such extras as compassion and humor and empathy and enthusiasm, so, when so it resembles humanoid in nature.

Oh, gotcha—"human-like".
We've been enlightened to ET crop circle art and now I'd like to ask about even stranger (and disturbing) events that have also been attributed to aliens: cow mutilations. Is this the doing of aliens, and if so why?

There have been such investigations as you mention, and this is the way of exploring what is in places visited. Curiosity of what is on your Earth plane only, and not considered with any emotion, simply a curious examination.

It is not to be repeated in the ways of past.

Well, I do consider it with emotion. Why cows?

Useful and purpose-built is the cow and it interests as this animal provides a substance, milk, which is the basis for many items in a healthy diet, and many more to become useful. Can it be replicated on another planet perhaps? Milks of varying types exist and from various plant sources are available.

(I'd imagine that ETs would surely be curious about why we breed and eat so many cows. "How strange," they must think.)

There are people who say that they were abducted by aliens. Have aliens indeed abducted some human beings, taken them aboard their ships, tested on them for a time, and then returned them? If so, why? According to the individuals who claim this experience, it was terrifying for them. In my view, this is a violation of an individual's free will and, if it has truly happened, we need to understand it while simultaneously

understanding aliens as friendly, which you have said they are.

The exploration of evolution of your Earth people is the curiosity leading to these incidences.

It is a fact there have been borrowings of Earth people for the purpose of inspection, close inspection in some cases, and this also was done out of curiosity and to document the human condition on your Earth at that time. It is the way of recording what is versus what has been and their record keeping extends to all things.

The buzzing by accomplishes some reconnaissance, but the close encounters are, or have been, utilized for deeper detail about humans on Earth.

Close encounters—I'd say!
Some of these alien abductees say that their DNA was taken for alien procreation, or that they were forced to have sex with aliens. Is any of this true?

The taking of DNA is simplistic but the sexual contact is less so. It would be against the norm and if investigation and examination of a deeper nature was required, perhaps it was so.

Procreation elsewhere by human standards is not a reality. The curiosity about methods for so doing attempts to be answered by close contact. It has been done and may be again, knowing it is research on the part of ETs for future consideration and species survival and flourishing.

Sometimes your answers require reading and re-reading. Like works of philosophy, they are for pondering.

Is this research for their own survival and flourishing, or is it related to the survival and flourishing of humans?

Oh yes, it is the ET future lifestyle survival. It is their interest in knowing all there is to know so they may apply as needed to their own culture. Procreation and ongoing life is a great concern and interest and curiosity drives their research. All is well in this and curiosity answered is curiosity resolved.

We say the reasons for human contact at any time are intended for long-term *good* as the divide between ETs and your human inhabitants of Earth narrows.

Remember that as your Earth people continue their intention and direction toward other planet colonization, there will be meeting and mixing: you will not be alone. You will be moving into another neighborhood and into another's territory where your rules do not always take priority and your per-ceived supremacy could be challenged, intellectu-ally for certain. Think on this.

Oh, I'm thinking on it, Pax.
How do aliens procreate? Let's go there.

They do not replicate the habits of your Earth people. To arrive fully formed and informed is their way. Wisdom is inherent.

I'm trying to imagine how a species procreates in a way in which they arrive fully formed.

Creation comes in many ways and to build in response to a need is one.

Birthing of an idea rather than birthing of a baby as is known on your plane—this is the way of it.

Okay, that's a concept that I can follow: the birthing of an idea.

Some, while not all, are created with a form of artificial intelligence that is hard to distinguish from what you consider humanoid—these are made, not born.

These workers referenced are created for specific purposes with what you would recognize as artificial intelligence.

Yes, you mentioned them.

These workers are created, made, not born, arriving task ready.

We speak of aliens as we have described, some leaders and some task-specific followers, some are hybrids and some not—this division remains.

There are variations on your inter-stellar traveling visitors where some look like you and others not even close and some in-between. Know that the many and varied reasons for being have created many and varied types of beings who inhabit other places, other planets in other galaxies, and other times. To equate these beings with humans is not always possible. Variations exist and in ways beyond explanation here. Similarly, Earth people vary according to location, climate, and lifestyle and your system of becoming differs greatly.

Why would some alien civilizations have developed this integration with artificial intelligence, such as these hybrids that you mention?

This is not the way of all future civilizations but has become known as a way of forming civilizations ready for all, as focus is on building and growing and upward planning and thinking in an intellectual and scientific manner. This is a way of going for some but not all. Others find themselves beginning closer to your Earthly norm. Nothing out there can be expected to parallel your Earthly way—it just is not the way.

Those neighbors from afar have streamlined their way of living and to function in what they consider the primitive way of Earth has long ago been left behind. Not only is your Earth primitive in your warring and divisiveness and hate and abuse and lack of respect for planetary resources, but it is primitive in the way of creating babies which are not self-sufficient for many Earth-years, not productive they say, and not conducive to moving quickly forward in development of life while all attention need focus on babies and children.

It does take us many years to grow up, get educated, and become ready to be on our purposes. Yet, as you know, we have no choice about this—it's just where we are in our evolution. *Or, do we have a choice?*

You don't, not at this point in your Earth time.

There are good things to be found in this way of growing and living that suit your purposes. Your civilization, on the whole, is not ready for the advanced ways we discuss so leave that for another time and place.

What do advanced interstellar beings eat? Of what does their diet consist?

Pure nutrients created from the highest source of pure and clean origins. It is a diet of nutrients rather than flavors, as you know it.

Do ETs have religion?

Religion as an organized and named following of people is archaic to them: where a book is considered eternal truth although it was created by humans not deities; legends and stories that dictate obedience in daily behavior and belief in what comes before and after life—these things are not considered by them as useful.

What are typical subjects of education in extra-terrestrial societies? Math, physics, telepathy …?

All is known by all and this is the way of it.

It is within the cells, this knowing, and extends to all aspects of the knowing of what is needed in their society.

To be arriving fully formed and initiated and educated, thus sparing the many years of growing in stature and knowledge—this is more efficient.

It is. And, it has me thinking of how much evolution we have yet to traverse. We'd better soon get past our pettiness and selfishness and greed and get on with the program!

I'd like to discuss the medical capabilities of ETs. Do they have advanced diagnostics or self-diagnostics? Is there disease in extraterrestrial communities? Are there hospitals on ET home bases?

Not in the usual form you are accustomed to in your spacetime. Their clean atmosphere and living spaces maintain a level of wellness you would wish for. Their wellness is disturbed occasionally but they have the ability to scan their bodies for dis-ease, identify it, and make change and improvement. Their ability to identify what is amiss and make change enables a very low level of unwellness to exist in their lives.

Also, their bodies don't resemble Earth people bodies and the internal function and systems are quite different and more easily fixed, improved, parts replaced and otherwise returned to wellness. It is a combination of parts replacement and repair. There will be more to come.

Oh, that's right, you have spoken about cloning and part replacement.

Many of our diseases are created by stress or made worse by stress and anxiety such as heart disease and high blood pressure to name a couple. Do aliens have stress?

Is it possible that stress is self-inflicted in your society? We say it is and can be managed as well as alleviated. This is an anxiety that is perpetrated upon your people by society and is not a requirement for happy life—it's detrimental in fact.

Off-Earth visitors do not accept this stress as a part of their make-up and it is non-existent. It is a choice, don't you know?

I agree that stress is a choice, one that's hard for us to shirk, yet it's still a choice.

Do extraterrestrials reincarnate as we do?

These ETs you refer to have a make-up that allows for repair and replacement of bodily components and they do not die as your Earth people know end of life to be. It is a continuum of life that they enjoy and being dis-ease free allows for this. Your life cycles seems primitive to them.

This again goes back to when we talked about cell memory and the ability to create new organs and body parts as needed, just as a salamander can grow a new tail.

But let's take a minute to clarify this to be sure that we have an accurate and full understanding. You told us about the ETs who were shot down at Roswell, New Mexico in 1947: the crew died in the crash, although one alien lived for a period but then died due to the testing our people conducted on it.

That being said, although they don't die from disease or old age, do ETs die if they are in an accident?

As has been stated, parts replacement and repair is the way, so continuation of being exists. If a situation exists such as Roswell and there isn't the opportunity to be "fixed"—end of operation and function is experienced.

In this rare situation where they meet an end, do they reincarnate and return to physicality again?

It is a replacement of their beings that occurs. They are complete in their journey. Others will be created to take their place and this creation is a result of a need: if there is no need, then no further creation.

This is not to be confused with reincarnation, for this does not take place in that society.

You have said that ET beings do indeed have souls—everything does. Therefore, if they do meet an end of their physicality, what happens to their soul? Do they simply remain in spirit after that?

There is a division in types of ET beings with some being operational and others being ongoing components of their individual societies.

There are workers that come and go and have end of cycle experiences: there is a full-circle experience where end of life is end of purpose and end of cycle—all is closed with gratitude. There isn't the ongoing continuation of soul in that dimension as you now know it.

While others are designed to go on and remain as leaders and therefore will continue.

Now we ask for you to understand the great divide between your understanding of what is, and what actually is. There needs to be no further explanation at this time. As your world turns and change comes to attitudes and warring becomes history, forward motion comes to exposure to off-planet lifestyles and the ability to assimilate. It is in the far time for your people.

Do ETs have team sports?

Do you consider team sport as it appears in inter-stellar craft racing and play around other galaxies as their way, then yes. Enjoyment is taken from activities useful to the many—there are no egos to feed.

Pax, this is too good to be true. We have had aliens completely wrong! Many people think of aliens as heartless, even violent, robotic, or purely cerebral. But they're fun-loving, joy-filled, and peaceful in intention.

Now, let's look at the lingering rumor of alien presence on Earth. There are people who say that in the foothills of the Andes mountains in the area of La Noria, Chile, there is a race of tiny human-like beings that scientists have called The Atacama Humanoid. For many hundreds of years, up to and including our present time, it is claimed that The Atacama Humanoid, a race of small people just six-inches tall, inhabits the land. They are referred to by some Chilean natives as "The Gentiles". Apparently, a well-preserved body was found and studied by a number of scientists not long ago.

Are "The Gentiles" a race that was Starseeded to Earth a very long time ago, like all of our races? Or, are they a much newer addition of what we would call aliens or intergalactic visitors of more recent times? Or, something else?

This is an unknown dimension in *human* races as they have come to be. Much like other anomalies of nature, one in history does not a species make.

Local legend and lore as known throughout your world history is often just that and based not on fact. Certainly, what lives there now is legend—truth is not known.

Some of our well-known space theorists say that the planet Sirius B, the companion to Sirius (the brightest star in our night sky, also known as the "Dog Star", located in the Canis Major constellation), is an *inhabited* planet. Is this true?

Inhabited by what, we ask? Certainly, many planets are found to have micro-life and this theory can be proven by the presence of moisture that supports life. Not rivers or oceans or lakes, but moisture that can descend from what, cloud? Not in *that* place. So what is it? Left over from eons past and held in place by the pressure exerted on the surface by external forces. So much to learn with so little return. Your people will not travel there.

Are there, now, other intelligent beings currently inhabiting any other planet in our Milky Way galaxy?

Oh yes, Penelope, it is the case that they are out there, and this will become more evident in time on your planet.

As your science and technology advances, and as your governments allow for that knowledge to be shared with the people, a new level of understanding the big picture will emerge. When the people are considered partners by science and government, there can be forward motion in thinking and acceptance. While they are being kept blindfolded and in fear of this type of progress, there can be no acceptance or willingness to contribute to the cause. Being a part of the solution is preferred, not part of the problem.

Using our most powerful telescopes, would it be possible to detect another star/planet that is inhabited?

Astronomers do their best and technology continues to allow for building more powerful telescopes, but proof of habitation does not come this way. Visitation and travel will confirm. There is much to be seen and learned, and technology struggles to keep up with need.

We suggest the way to create more powerful viewing is through Remote Viewing. We have discussed this but not in the context of off-planet exploration—think on it.

That is a compelling suggestion.
It's a big galaxy. In what arm of the Milky Way galaxy is there a planet inhabited by intelligent beings?

In the time of ancients in your solar system there was much buzzing about in travel to explore other places. It was found that there are reasons to explore, as life exists in different forms elsewhere out there. These forms are advanced or not and vary widely from single cell to intellectual and scientific and advanced—all support one another and function independently of their off-planet cousins.

This circulation of energy throughout the star system was and is and continues to be. In another time on your Earth more will be known. What is to be is the veil of secrecy lifted and open travel and visitation, but as long as your Earth people consider space as something to be monetized and claimed, it cannot be without cataclysmic results. So, time must pass while saner heads prevail, and openness and inclusion of space travel and its consequences begins.

I can imagine that we could learn much about Higher Self attainment if we studied the lives and cultures of ETs. Do they regularly operate from their Higher Self as a common and natural way of functioning?

These beings *are* their Higher Selves as they function on a level of spirituality unknown to your people. Theirs is civilization advanced in all ways and we say it is to be emulated, and will be in time, your Earth time.

Meanwhile, growth and understanding of higher functioning is a goal. Your civilization has much to learn of peace and equality—begin there.

How can we emulate our friendly intergalactic supporters if we don't know them?

To become a spiritual being is the way. Your people shall begin to know themselves and what they may do to know their Higher Selves. The functioning at a higher level of spirituality is the beginning— it is the way to advance the cause and that cause is elevation of functioning of all people—to consider the big picture, remove hatred and become inclusive; do not consider personal needs above all else. Consider others and consider the needs of Mother Earth as a higher calling. You all are spiritual beings having a human experience. Some do it better than others.

While ETs *are* their Higher Selves, do they continue to evolve their Higher Selves?

They bring to their collective the walking of the talk and living in the light of purity. One monitors another and their civilization dwells in the light—it is expected and enjoyed and provides the cocoon of wellness created by them for them. Higher technology is a part of their world and this in no way interferes with the overall view they have of their purpose for being: to continue evolution and education.

So, they are their Higher Selves and their purpose is their continued evolution and education. This kind of purpose is one that can be understood by those on Earth who are dedicated to our spiritual evolution and the studies of metaphysics, Higher Self development, and other vocations of science, knowledge, and truth seeking. However, many other people on Earth today would not be able to relate to this course of enlightenment as their *entire* reason for being. Many do not dedicate their lives to the quest for knowledge or the honing of talents and skills in any field. Many believe that their lives are about simple pleasures, survival, success as demonstrated through financial milestones, or how far up the corporate ladder they are able to climb. The latter (and ladder) group might find a lifelong quest for evolution and education to be dull or unsatisfactory.

May you please speak to how and why these other advanced and enlightened civilizations (ETs and OPAs) grew to rank their spirituality and dissemination of knowledge as their top priority and purpose for being?

Ah yes, it is age—that is, age of their *societies*. It is said that age brings wisdom, is it not? And it is the case that they long ago left behind the level of chaos your civilization currently experiences. This comes with generations of change and how you describe many among your people now as unwilling to devote their lives to a quest for evolution, so be it:

they will be replaced through attrition by those who will and do—it is the way of it.

We say that the shift in thinking and acting is now beginning. Although nowhere near a tipping point in your society, the surge has begun. When it becomes a tsunami will be within two generations and your people may be considered wise.

At their advanced level, what are the practices of other galactic society's peoples in terms of Higher Self development and spiritual maintenance?

Living it is the way. Alternatives are not known. It is the joy of being in the bliss.

What is "the bliss"? Many people experience happiness, yet not "bliss". Perhaps those people who experience bliss do so during moments of meditation, or when their child is born, or when they first tasted chocolate as a child, or when their sports team wins, or when they reach a goal such as summiting a formidable mountain, or another feat of physical, spiritual, or mental exuberance—yet these are periodical and not a steady state of living.

It would be greatly appreciated if you will help us to understand what bliss is, *where* it is, and what it feels like.

Bliss is to be found within your heart and mind. It is the knowing feeling of love in all things, wellness in all things, and harmony in all things. Imagine that and work toward it in your own life: this is our suggestion for your people at this time. It's even better than chocolate. Trust in this and accept it with love as intended.

You're kind of cheeky sometimes. ("*Better than chocolate*.")

To briefly sidetrack, is humor a thing in the *Spirit World*?

Have we not indicated in our words and manner of approaching some topics that we indeed have this in our make-up?

Yes, you have.

All is not serious, all is not reverence, all is an amalgam of ways and to enjoy the serendipity and humor displayed forms a part.

Dear Divine Wisdom Source, I'm thrilled to hear that you have a sense of humor. In guiding us, no doubt you need one.

On a more serious note—you know, the day will come that the people of Earth are made aware of the existence of ETs and the visitations by our friendly interstellar supporters. This event is called Alien Disclosure, and it refers to a time or moment when our governments formally acknowledge the presence of ETs—all is divulged.

How soon from now will Disclosure happen? And why? Does something happen whereby our governments are left with no option but to admit to what they have known for some time?

If you ask about *time* we are at a disadvantage, as we do not know your linear measure. What brings about a disclosure would be mass visitation, but this would not be undertaken as your military would be called to order and hostility ensues. Your people are unprepared in their knowledge and trust and have been kept in this way deliberately to ensure Government maintains control.

That's unfortunate.

Our governments (and many people) worry about being attacked by ET visitors. Are there extraterrestrial visitors—any at all, anywhere of any race of beings—that would intend to harm us, war with us, or take over our planet? (I have asked this before and am taking another go to be sure.)

These interstellar tourists *could have* done any amount of harm over the last thousands of years had they wished to. It is not their intention now or ever.

It is to be known that action brings reaction, and should they be met with assault rifles, what do you think may be the reaction? There is much education to be undertaken among your people and there is no showing of readiness at this time.

We suggest that when the tsunami comes and your people are more enlightened and accepting of the reality of global healing and interstellar travel, there will be those ready to accept and manage the next phase of welcoming and inclusion.

We currently do not have any protocol for a post-disclosure world—at least not one of which the people are aware. Rather than waiting for a plan of defense and offense to be presented to us by our world governments, many people would like to get a protocol that we can all start to think about. What should be our guidelines of diplomacy with ETs? Can you give us a set of parameters that should be followed in our interactions?

The people of Planet Earth are not prepared, at this time, for consideration of what you suggest. Rigidity and fear in mindset prevails and it is ludicrous to think that sending out lessons of peaceful interaction expected is going to calm the nature of those expecting the worst. There are world leaders already speaking of weaponizing space, claiming territory, and becoming masters of those new universes. It is not in their planning to share and be respectful of those with higher technology landing in peace. It will not happen in your generation or some to follow. There must be further understanding of the need for peace and respect for all and combining resources for the greater good.

You are really driving this point home and I'm sure we need the repetition on this matter to get the message. Please continue.

As there are multiple nationalities together in a space capsule at the International Space Station, and they work together for the growth and success of the space program, so should your countries work together to consider the ramifications of life on other planets and what they can learn that may assist in the healing of Planet Earth.

More is to be learned and shared while continuing to refer to those from other planets wishing to bring peace.

There will not be opportunity for interaction in person until your world has taken many turns and change has come to your attitude and intention for control. When there will be interaction, respect and peaceful intention must be presented.

Releasing fear in people only comes through knowledge, and there will not be a sufficient growth of knowledge while the visitors distance themselves. The beginning is within your Earth people's culture to change the way of thinking, send the communication of this by the telepathic means of communication that will be common, and begin to function in peace and love. Only then, will it be noticed that a shift has taken place and perhaps it is time, once again, to entertain the notion of landing on Earth. As stated, another generation or two will grow in their enlightenment before this event.

On this topic, please speak directly to our political world powers.

As your people speak of space exploration and begin to consider funding more of it, there is talk of claiming territory and planning to weaponize space. What is this thinking and how does it represent purity of intention and peaceful growth in knowledge? We are saddened by this that the first thought, it would seem, is to politicize the next frontier, space, and begin with the thought of claiming and staking territory and meeting inhabitants of other planets with weapons. How is this any different from the current attitude of Earth countries' politicians?

To war and to conquer is what got you into this difficulty. Do you think that to begin space exploration with this attitude is the way forward? Clearly you do and therefore will receive no assistance from those of higher civilizations that could pave the way for your success.

You will witness failures where there need not be and losses that were preventable. Your unwillingness to go in peace is your great weakness and your point of failure. You are to consider this mentality to be less, not more, in the overall measure of mankind, and you are shameful in this attitude.

Foresight is what is lacking now in your population involved in this sector, and foresight will be needed. As you look through a limited vision hole, much like closing one eye or turning your binocular backward, the goal seems distant and difficult to achieve. Much more introspection and clarity of thinking is required.

That was direct. Hopefully those who need to hear are listening.

What is our test to pass or benchmark of enlightenment that will signal to you and the Spirit World that we have tapped into our Higher Selves, that we can be trusted with future wisdoms and technologies, and that we are ready and have earned the opening of our next passage?

Purity of intention is the answer here.

This is in the minority now and will not tip the scales into the majority for a long while. There are those among you now fitting this description. There is a small segment of your population with the passion for this endeavor and they are to be enabled to continue this pursuit: It is an idea whose time has come. They are the learners and researchers and believers and quiet revolutionaries who plan for the interstellar travel mentioned. It is their purity of intention that singles them out for not only their work, but their successes along their path. As they work on propulsion for space travel, they quietly know the way and continue to process the steps required to bring it to fruition.

When it is determined by your science and politics that peaceful exploration of space is the way, without weapons and territorial attitudes, progress will be made toward safe and successful travel.

For your people to understand why they wish to visit off-planet or colonize off-planet—and how that will look in terms of spirituality, is needed. This is the foresight that comes from looking within and mining one's own internal wisdom. Each involved has higher powers and old souls that carry much wisdom—it is this that is to be mined.

Do not ask without, ask *within* for your guidance and foresight is found.

Chapter Twenty-Nine

A Place in Time

*M*y wish for this conversation is that we learn how to get from where we are to where we want to be in the journey of our consciousness awakening and spiritual evolution.

We see that there are those in fear of traveling without a map or a hand to guide them. There will be those who lead and those who follow, of course, but the road less traveled is the right one for many.

The road less traveled is a nice toss, as we say in television. Let's get on it. I'll let you go first. What shall we discuss?

It is indeed the case that there is a linear time thinking process among your people, and yet this is not the way.

Excellent, we'll talk about the subject of time. *It's a tickin'.*

It is all in a box and at the same time and can be accessed at will. The notion that one is gone and another not yet reached is incorrect. It is all one and you may move from one to the other readily.

One what is gone? Are you speaking of *moments in time*?

Moments, sections of time, spaces of time and place: all are simultaneous in their existence. Thinking your way from one into the other is the way. Much like teleporting it is the will that enables the transition. We share with you that it is the intention coupled with the idea that creates this reality.

This is a notion that is difficult for some to process, but it is, and it will be understood by many others. It brings excitement, does it not?

It sure does. Are you really saying that we can access all possibilities at will, and that nothing is in the past or future that we can't access now?

This is what we have said.

You are capable of visiting this idea and trying it out for yourself. It's like climbing a wall in that if you believe you can do so, you will, but if you stop believing part way up, you may lose your grip and fall. Inner trust is your power.

Do future peoples exist on Earth in some realm now?

The notion of "parallel universes" is one that can and has been experienced by the enlightened. It is a place and time where life exists and does so at a different pace and in a higher frequency than Planet Earth as you know it. As fascinating as this seems to many, it is reality. Future Earth civilizations will develop from both sources and as is the case now, some will move between these realms and bring back extraordinary knowledge and experience; they will be the leaders. This is the current situation, but those individuals are looked upon as intellectually superior and not spiritually advanced; both happen to be reality.

Oh, this is so interesting. Can I learn to move between these realms to bring back extraordinary knowledge? If so, how might I do this?

One step at a time, now, and the work you are doing is of value and needed in your place and time.

Is there a reason that you put "parallel universe" in quotes? Is there a *better* term that we could begin using? And, you say that parallel universes have been experienced by the enlightened: are these enlightened people from another time or from another place?

All of the above: from Earth, from another time and another place, and the term is parallel universe. It is somewhat widely known and experienced by those who pass between realities for higher purposes. It is a place, a thing, and has in our view, a proper name.

Do we affect those parallel universes? Do the current occurrences on Earth affect another, or many, versions of Earth in other times and places and space?

We say those parallel universes are what they are, in time, and function independently of Earth people and time now. To the extent that some pass back and forth between your present and those other times and places, there is a touching, therefore an effect, but it is a portal that opens for some and closes behind them. To pass between realms is done voluntarily or also involuntarily where the portal opens and access is given unexpectedly. It is a surprise at times but always a reason appears as valid for that person's lifetime experience, one or both. Teaching and learning continues and growth between these universes is the reason for such visitations. Working toward enlightenment, those who travel have contributions to make and lessons to learn along the way.

What's the purpose of parallel universes?

We do not identify a parallel universe as having a purpose but rather it is a place, a "like life" existence where the choices you have made in this life play out there differently, alternatively, as the choices you did not make here with those differing results becoming apparent.

It is an awareness of what might have been. It is an existence, another dimension in time that one can slip in and out of as through a portal.

Wow—just, wow!

If every choice and action has a life and path in another universe, then there must be millions—no, trillions—of universes.

I wonder if there must be *countless* other universes. Is that right?

Not every choice and action plays out in another universe. It is not so complicated. Countless other parallel universes are as those who choose to visit allow.

This is for the few, not the many.

Oooh.

In all other universes, is there a "me" as I know me; a me of which my soul is conscious?

No and this is not the way of it. Your choice would be for one.

For one what? One soul, or one awareness of one Universe?

Yes, both. Envision a room divided by a curtain. On one side you act in a play as one character and on the other you return to your daily self and lifestyle. You are one person living two separate lives and as you pass through the curtain portal your life awaits and you resume activity. You are one soul living parallel lifetimes, each drawing you in for different actions and activities and you may leave each for the other at will.

This analogy is very helpful.

By way of those vastly variant choices, do I have a different name, personality, appearance, and/or even a different soul history in other universes?

There can be a difference in most of these including place in time in history. There is a learning component to why a visit is undertaken. Learning of life preferences and choices for future, and which suits going forward.

Of all of the "MEs", could it be said that I am simply all persons and therefore every person is me and I am every person?

No.

While all of these many parallel universes are exactly as the name implies, are they also just one Life in that all is connected?

No. A different life or lifetime in each universe allows for information gathering and experiences and relationships to merge and determine which life to continue and on which universe time and place. It is an offering of what may be and what could have been. Slipping between and through portals allows for this and is for a reason and for the few.

Are parallel universes different places in terms of spacetime coordinates or physical locations?

The notion of parallel universe is an alternative for those who access a place in their wishes and dreams and is not a given for all people. It is magical and mystical and allows for those who place themselves there to see both sides of a life and how it might have been if other choices were made. One may travel back and forth and learn from both. Ultimately, a choice will be made, and one lifetime may become the forever choice and staying with it and the associated people will be the end result.

I think I understand this better now.
Let's discuss time. Why does the Spirit World not operate within linear time?

We do not know that fixation on time; ours is a differing place and linear time is non-existent. It has to do with many facets of being non-solid in make-up. Ours is a way of being and not a moderated example of what science likes to manage. Ours is fluid and not captured in your astrophysical ways.

Did our relationship with linear time begin when we were Starseeded to Earth?

Linear time is yours and is based on planetary rotation. It is the way of your world.

You must understand that time travel, teleportation, and lightspeed travel also are not measured in a timeframe your people would comprehend. Think of time as a *place* not a measure of distance.

This will be mind-blowing for many people. But wait, you also said that Dark Energy is a place. (Any correlation, I wonder?) You said, *"Separate time from place from intelligence and it will be clear."* Let me probe further.

I'm trying to think of time as a place; can you further describe this to make the concept understandable for us?

If you were to put a box around a picture of where you are now—it is a place. If you repeat this process the next day, it is also a place shown in that picture. However, each is a place but in a different time— a different day—a same place in a different time. These are places in time. They show time in place.

I've just been out for a walk in the sun and I kept thinking of the boxes around the place, and how tomorrow it will be the same location—different time, of course—but now a different place

in time. It can go on and on into infinity with that visualization.

Let's take our discussion of time up into space. Can space–time be folded like a sheet? If so, as it's folded, can two portals or pathways that were light years apart become folded into the same place? Does this make travel instantaneous between far off points in the Universe?

Oh yes, it is the way of it and the magic, also. When it is managed this way there can be teleportation in an instant. Think of that! Your world becomes a different place when this becomes known. Of course, at this time in your development you need a welcoming destination for earthlings and that will take some time to achieve. It comes.

When we colonize another planet, how will we count time or relate to time in that other place? After all, we use a twenty-four-hour system which is based on the Earth's revolutions around the sun. Therefore, what counting system will be used in other places with other suns and moons and so on?

You must know that all is relative to location and the structure of your twenty-four-hour method will not apply elsewhere. Your people who begin space travel in experiments will cling to this as a measure of progress, initially, and soon become aware of alternatives to this earthly way.

Evolution will take your people from Earth dwellers to off-planet explorers, and in that will evolve a need for new ways of tracking periods of travel and habitation. These are determined by locations and will serve your people well as they adjust to their growth as inhabitants of new worlds.

When in Rome, it is said, and in this new way of being the way will be found along with the place in time.

In past discussions, you have mentioned teleportation. I recall we talked about the disappearance of the Mayans and the transport of the stones of the Stonehenge circle and the Great Pyramids. Can you "tip us off" as to how we can make the jump in knowledge and technology to achieve the teleportation of products and people? What insight can you share regarding teleportation?

Teleportation is a thought process; an escalation of the mind over matter way. It is not a trick of physics but rather an intention.

Oh, so teleportation is not done like in Star Trek (with computers and instruments that deconstruct then reconstruct cellular patterns), and it's not done through the laws of physics by way of particles in quantum entanglement?

Deconstruct, reconstruct, think it with intention and visualization and it is. Also required is belief in this as possibility; infinite possibility.

You practice and function using the power of intention, and this is no different. To dissolve in one area and reappear in another; this is the speed at which one moves accounting for the illusion.

What's "the illusion"?

It is the illusion of being there one moment and then disappearing, or magically appearing in a place where you were not a moment ago. The illusion is that you weren't there the whole time.

That last sentence is one to ponder.
And what is astral travel?

This is simply the mind leaving the Earth body to travel to other places, perhaps other planets and galaxies, then returning to the body. It is often a sleep-originated practice where one visits elsewhere and returns with great or even profound experiences.

Can you teach us how to do it?

There are many books on this subject and learning the full aspect and ramifications to be considered are to be learned there. It is not a game and is to be considered fully prior to undertaking. Read and learn and decide—some who do this do not find their way back to the body in time for it to be still viable.

Yikes.

Others have brief sojourns resulting in increased knowledge—it is to be respected, this ability.

Do our friendly interstellar visitors return to learn from Earth herself?

In terms of their time of existence and past assimilation and learning, their purpose is to guide and teach. They do so from a distance while remaining obscure, usually.

It is your Earth people also who pass through the portals and return in a leading of a double life. Lessons to teach and learn, and if they alternate this is the way of it. Who is on the other side differs for each one's experience and is specific to their experiences and needs. Nothing is forever in these scenarios, and they serve their purpose and the portal closes.

It is a whimsical thing and contributes greatly to growth of Spirit.

What exactly are "the portals"? What does a portal look like and how does it appear?

A portal is a place not a thing and doesn't have a look. It is an opening in time only and not relegated to one place. Like a brief parting of a closed curtain, it allows passage between time and place. It is quite magical and is experienced by those who look for it as well as those unsuspecting who have a need and are given the gift of it.

That's right, you have told us that American pilot and adventuress Amelia Earhart traveled through a time-portal!

May you tell us more about time travel as a process of thinking?

Time travel is a *result*.

This is a big stretch for us. We don't yet believe that our thoughts are this powerful—powerful enough to result in travel through time. We know the concepts of our will, our intention, and our ideas, yet maybe you can help us out a little more because we're not practiced in using these tools in the capacity of time travel.

How can we take our willpower to that level?

We say your "willpower" is quite separate from this discussion. It is inner trust in self—belief in self to the exclusion of all else—that is to be further strengthened. It is intention combined with this trust in self and Self that powers you on your desired path. It is also purity of intention that completes the fueling of your journey.

I'd like to try this out, as you have suggested. I'd like to better understand this ability because I'm not sure that I do.

Let's run through a trial to find out if it is what I think it is and how it can work. First, I'll describe a moment in time that is in the future.

Here's the hypothetical example:

A replacement material to plastics-made-of-crude-oil has been discovered. As you told us, it is a composition of hemp cellulose together with other renewable and reusable plant-based ingredients. In fact, this moment is possible because our writings have been read by so many around the world and now people are aware of the possibility. The demand is creating the supply of this new material—let's say it's called "plantic". I choose to make purchases that support my vision for a clean Earth, and so, I go online to buy a set of plantic food storage containers, plantic food wrap, plantic straws and cups for an upcoming party that I'm hosting, and plantic baby bottles as a gift for a friend.

Okay, let's press pause on that moment. How can I actually buy those items when in the now they don't yet exist? And, if this is not the way to journey to this future place-in-time, or perhaps the future is *not* accessible in this tangible way, then please further explain this "result".

> It is not the way of now to move those items from a future time to now in that you envision going to a future store to purchase them.

It is rather the way that these things do exist in *that* time period where you may find yourself and your experience of seeing and using those futuristic items would take place in that place in time.

If this is a parallel universe, so be it, but when you pass through the portal on return you will come back to what is *here* and in existence *now*, speaking of your Planet Earth. You will not move a futuristic washing machine through the portal because you wish to—but you may experience it on the other side and you may generate the idea for how it can be created on your Earth plane of existence in your present place in time.

You may live and learn, as it is said, and return with ideas and details and methods with which to replicate what you saw. This is the way of it.

It is being transported from place in time to place in time: a warp and a dissolution of solid, molecules disappearing and regrouping. We spoke of voice-commands morphing into thought commands—this is it but on a greater scale.

All right, time is a result and a place. When reading between the lines, I think that the meaning of "place in time" might be "place in place". So then, time does not exist, only places exist. Is this accurate?

If you listen to musical notes between the lines, between the notes, there will be a distortion of meaning. There are places in time and space, and all exist. To be in a place in time is to be in *motion*: life moves as time moves and places occupied pass between and through. It is fluid, this time, and so be it.

I imagine these snapshots of time in motion— like a motion picture; a reel; a film. I'm really getting this now!

In order for us to master teleportation, is the challenge purely one of mastering thought commands, or do we need to overcome time in some way?

Oh hah, to overcome time is not a requirement, rather to work with it and go with the flow, as it is said, contributes to this process. One must not be confrontational when one can be a contributor to the process and success of it.

Be one with the Universe.

Yes, yes! Go with the flow. Be one with the Universe. We didn't just make these lines up, huh? (A rhetorical question; we know the answer here.)

Is time teleportation and time travel the same thing?

Is this a philosophical question? To teleport from place A to place B moves the body, but did it really pass through time or arrive at a different time? Only if that place in time is located elsewhere.

Consider airplane travel on your world today. You may travel for hours but arrive yesterday. It's all relative. You will arrive at a different place in time, yes? Should you wish to travel to another century past—this is a different place in time where you may experience what was.

Time varies throughout the Universe, but time is and is a required link in the chain of Universal wellbeing. Many are those who state that time is not a link required to survive, but time is survival for without it there is no survival.

"Your time is up" is a long-standing expression meaning when you cease to exist. Think on this and understand the connection.

It's all beginning to resonate and I'm gaining a new perspective on time and place.

Imagine if you will, the technology race now compounded by the passage of time and advances in technology. It boggles the mind, it does.

Imagine also that the technology that you now find state of the art is obsolete. What do you envision will replace it? Do you have any idea in the changes of your methods of communication and traveling? It will look like a different place and civilization entirely.

We are here to say that the time comes when the next generation is approaching the age of majority, when what you now take for granted is wiped clean away from the operative methods currently known.

Well, that is what is coming, and you should be prepared to accept the transition although some already understand and see the future.

What is the fifth dimension that I've read about in metaphysical teachings?

There are dimensions in existence that mimic waves like ripples of time.

In your current third dimension living you have the sights and the sounds and the thinking of what is.

In the fifth dimension of living you have all of that plus the intuitive and the enlightened gifts of life in your abilities.

While you are very happy and contented now without the knowledge of what is possible, you will be ecstatic in the experience of more.

"Ecstatic" is a powerful word. I want to vicariously feel that ecstasy through your words. May you please tell me a story of life in the fifth dimension? What is possible and what are our abilities in that dimension?

What can you imagine? What do you wish for? What brings happiness? For some it is prosperity and for others love, and yet others consider the elevation of their daily life over the present work and need to earn a living a form of life management. All are to be, of course, as the journey toward enlightenment will show.

Entering this place of your future will bring peace and harmony and is found through the evolution of your own way of thinking and being. Finding enlightenment of spirit is a journey and your civilization is not there yet; not even both feet on the path, as it were.

To be in this realm of all possibilities is meaning your purity of spirit brings purity of thought and action toward all things, people, and animals on your planet, and your intention is honorable toward all. A day in the life here is peace and purity and as though travelling with feet on clouds of goodness. All forward motion toward continued planetary wellness is agreed upon and managed quietly and with good intention toward all, as we have stated, and this overriding belief touches all aspects of life and living.

The fifth dimension sounds incredible. Although, I suppose we've skipped one: is there a fourth dimension and, if so, what is it and how do we bridge our path from the third to the fourth?

Ah yes, development of your people and the journey toward enlightenment brings this about. For your people to have realization that their "this" is not all they have or should strive for is a beginning.

We wish to show that all have the opportunity to grow in their spirituality and grow in their gifts and talents for spiritual journeys. To use their gifts for the betterment of others puts them on track for their higher evolution and to know they strive for increased awareness and ability to practice their talents also places them ahead of their present sedentary existence.

Growing in knowledge and purity of spirit is this next step and understanding their role as student and then teacher, completes the stages. To be blessed with the ability to learn and grow and then gift this to others is the journey for many, and as a journey, it feels like a gift.

The true gift is in practicing the new ways of higher living and higher learning and placing respect for all and purity of intention above all else.

This is our gift to you.

Going forward from here I wonder how our intentions and actions will shape our future. Let's go on a time travel journey of sorts.

Will we have the Internet in fifty years, or will it be something else? If so, what?

Oh my, this will look very different as will be the devices used to access. All will be connected through an energy field you can tap into, or not, and access all information and desired communication.

What will social media be like in fifty years?

Not a separate entity or entities as now, but a component of the central reality of communication through the Ethernet: all is one and one is all—it becomes an integral part of the whole which is the communication channels developed to carry all wisdom.

I guess the folks at Facebook and Twitter will want to diversify.

In fifty years, will moviemaking and movie-watching still be as popular as it is today?

It will but in a very different format. People will not sit in theatres when they can access all media as they move about and download all to their internal chip and view it as if they are in a hologram. It is a departure from your current ways.

That sounds very cool—we'll be *in* the movie.

If we changed nothing of our ways, attitudes, governments, and industry practices, and continued on our current trajectory, what would life on Planet Earth be like in just *ten* years?

Very dark in all respects: the beginning of the death of the planet which has already begun, but effectively crippling the means of growing clean crops as clean air, water, and soil are non-existent.

How about in fifty years?

Government would look very differently as corruption would have melded current major countries into others who rule by fear and manage as dictatorships.

Earth is polluted to the extent that food sources are no longer viable.

Off-planet travel is common, territories were claimed there, and war begins for dominance in space.

Very unpleasant.

On the flip side, if we implemented all of your suggestions and wisdom, and began now to follow our hearts, trust in our selves, stand up to government and industry corruption, and be the change we wish to see—what would life on Planet Earth be like in ten years?

There would be a resurgence of the need to leave fossil fuel production, limit waste into air and water and manage the Earth resources as did the aboriginal and First Nations before you.

Peace begins to be felt among world powers and it is felt that the world's people wish to support each other in finding the best place for each in their development.

And, then again, in fifty years?

Your planet will be more quiet: there is not the warring that has been in history and the feeling of peace prevails in all things.

There are bumps in the road still but the driving force in industry and government is to take the direction of clean and quiet and good for all.

Love prevails.

Imagine.

Trust in this and go in Peace and Love.

—Pax.

About the Author and Channeler

*P*enelope Jean Hayes is a new consciousness author, television personality, and speaker. She has appeared on-camera hundreds of times as an expert guest on programs including *Dr. Phil*, *ABC News*, as well as international news specials and telecasts. She is the foremost leader in the field of contagious and osmotic energy known as Viralenology, founder of the Viral Energy Institute, and author of the book *The Magic of Viral Energy: An Ancient Key to Happiness, Empowerment, and Purpose.*

Carole Serene Borgens channels Pax, the Divine Wisdom Source. Carole is a former nurse and longtime student of metaphysics. She has been channeling Spirit since the early 1990s when she was chosen by Pax and given the title "Spirit Messenger". Carole continues to write and provide in-person and remote sessions for clients around the globe, and she refers to her gift of channeling as "the greatest blessing in my life."

Of this trio, Pax says, "A good team we three."

www.PaxWisdom.com
www.PenelopeJeanHayes.com
www.CaroleSereneBorgens.com